ALLEN PHOTOGRAPHIC GUIDES

FIELD MANAGEMENT FOR HORSES AND PONIES

CONTENTS

WHY IS FIELD MANAGEMENT NECESSARY?

The quality of grazing and the nutritional requirements of the horse vary considerably throughout the year, and rarely complement each other. With careful management, it is possible to minimise the differences in this imbalance of nutritional need and grazing supply and to stabilise the quality and health of the pasture, thereby maximising the existing grazing facilities. The usage, type and quality of the existing grazing must be assessed, with consideration of other variables affecting the land, such as climate and temperature, soil pH and consistency, drainage and the make-up of the existing grass sward.

GRAZING AND PASTURE

IDEAL GRAZING

The ideal grazing for horses is a species-rich grassland which provides a resilient sward. Old meadows and pastures make good grazing as they are rich in minerals and contain a mix of beneficial herbs, such as fescue. Clover is another useful herb as it is a natural 'fixer' of beneficial nitrogen in the soil and is resilient to drought, although not necessarily to other extreme conditions. Such pasture is highly valuable as it provides excellent hay. To assess the existing composition, you must be able to recognise the desirable grass and herb species and estimate the relative proportions of these against problem weeds such as docks, thistles and ragwort. If you are fortunate to

have access to this type of good grassland, be aware that it needs continued grazing and hay-making to prevent it from being overtaken by bramble and scrub.

THE UNSUITABLE FIELD

Grass that has been used for grazing cattle, particularly beef cattle, is usually lush and rich in fattening carbohydrates

KNOW YOUR GRASS

Learn to identify whether the pasture is lush cattle pasture or is valuable old meadow pasture.

(a significant cause of laminitis), although it tends to be free from worms. Lush cattle pasture is likely to cause a notable and dangerous increase in weight, causing a swollen grass belly. It is also important to check for rough, uneven ground and rabbit holes, which may go unnoticed in long grass.

If your land is unsuitable, avoid ploughing up and reseeding it if at all possible, unless it is already a short-term lay, i.e. less than five years old. Ploughing releases nutrients, may cause leaching of the soil and destroys valuable organic matter which is beneficial for both the soil and the horses' legs. Oversowing and careful management have been found to be a better solution.

SEASONAL CONSIDERATIONS

One of the worst aspects of winter for most horse owners is the badly poached fields caused by horses gathering in boggy areas on which the grass cannot survive. Heavy rain leaches fertility from bare soil, recently fertilised grassland, or very steep grassland, and any remaining grazing will therefore be low in nutrients.

Spring brings with it a flush of carbohydrate-rich, nutritious grass and, if over indulgence is allowed, the horse is unwittingly subjected to a higher risk of obesity and laminitis. It has been shown that keeping the grass short actually increases its productivity, so cutting lush grass down will in fact provide more and richer nutrients. It is therefore preferable to maintain a longer sward of no more than 6 cm, where the grasses have matured and are no

longer growing thick and fast, although intake should still be restricted. A low-productivity semi-natural sward would be most suitable for laminitic horses and ponies.

Good weather towards the end of the summer, usually early September, may induce a second flush of grass. This may be long and filling, but it is of lower nutritional value than the first spring flush. If you have other grazing, from September on is an ideal time to rest your best grazing. Turning horses out too soon onto new, tender grass growth will risk ruining the grazing for the year ahead. This also applies to the spring flush.

AVOIDING PASTURE PROBLEMS

Pasture problems can be avoided, or at least minimised, with a little foresight, preparation and careful management. Horses are fussy grazers, selecting short grass over long patches. Consequently, areas of rough, dank, poor quality grass are left untouched and are used for defecation, leading to the growth of problem weeds such as thistles and docks. This pattern will soon become cyclical if manure is not regularly removed.

Pick up droppings daily to reduce the worm burden and encourage even grazing. If you have a large area of land to keep clear, it may be worth investing in a horse muck collector, some of which even collect grass clippings and leaves.

If many horses are grazing on the same pasture all year round, the ground will become horse sick. The nutritional content of overgrazed grass is low and the horse is

likely to lose condition unless his diet is supplemented. Divide the grazing into two or more paddocks, preferably three, so that land is rested, treated and grazed in rotation. One can be used for horses, one rested and one for grazing sheep or cattle which graze the overgrown patches and even eat weeds that horses avoid.

ROOM TO THRIVE

As a guide, you need an acre of land per horse plus one extra acre.

GRAZING OTHER LIVESTOCK

Ask your local farmer if you can swap grazing. Turn your horse out on a farmer's valuable old pasture when your horse grazing is poor and lacking in nutrition and, in return, the farmer's sheep or cattle can be put onto your horse grazing when it is too rich and lush. Check that the farmer's land is free from poisonous plants before giving your horse unlimited access.

NATURAL WORMERS

Cattle are resistant to the species of worms that affect horses, and thus act as a natural wormer on equine pasture.

Dividing the pasture makes it possible to isolate a horse if necessary, for reasons such as temperament, injury or illness. It also allows for the creation of a 'starvation paddock' in which the grazing is kept to a minimum for horses with a tendency to put on weight. Horses on smaller paddocks on which grazing is limited will be less fussy about where they graze and are more likely to eat poisonous plants, so make daily checks.

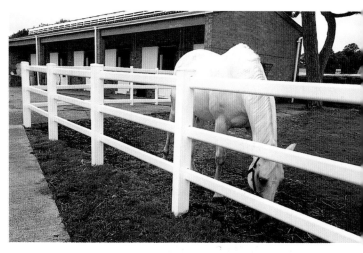

By dividing the pasture during the winter, you can select the driest paddock for wet weather use. Examine the drainage carefully to identify which paddock drains most freely. If the ground is very wet, graze the horses on the least valuable land, as it is more susceptible to damage in this condition.

DRAINAGE

INDICATORS OF POOR DRAINAGE

- Surface water

- Plants such as rushes, tussock and couch grass, and buttercups.

Poaching The most poached areas of the field tend to be around the gate, water troughs, feeding areas and field shelters: areas where horses congregate or frequently pass through. You can prevent or minimise poaching by covering the area with a layer of limestone or quarry stone. (*see opposite page, top*)

DRAINAGE SOLUTIONS

A long-term solution to poached ground is to remove the soil in the problem area down to the subsoil, and then replace it with a layer of sand or cinders to provide drainage that is more effective. A combination of protective covering and effective drainage from the area is the ideal solution.

A common cause of surface water is blocked boundary ditches and outlets, so the first step is to make sure these are cleared. Where underground channels or drainage pipes need to be installed, professional advice from a reputable company should be sought.

Avoid feeding and watering horses at the same place in the field every day. Ensure water troughs are not leaking or unstable. If you have to water your horse from a standard water bucket, place it in two suitably sized tyres to prevent it from being kicked over and flooding the proximity. During the summer when the ground is parched and dry, graze horses on land that has slightly poorer drainage as it will retain water and therefore have a more nutritious sward in dry conditions.

THE SOIL

SOIL TYPES

There are two main types of soil, that which has a high percentage of **clay** and that which has a higher percentage of **sand**.

Soil with a high clay content (*see below*) appears to be heavier, poaches easily and will need good drainage, although it has the advantage of being highly fertile even in dry weather.

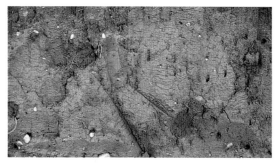

Soil with a high sand content (*see below*) will be lighter and drain relatively well, but it is lower in nutrients.

Grass growth is controlled largely by temperature and will start earlier in the year on warmer, south facing slopes. Lighter soil warms up quickly and therefore tends to dry out quickly in the summer, causing the ground to harden earlier in the year as the soil warms. Fertiliser may also be leached away from lighter soils. Heavier soil takes longer to warm up and consequently grass growth will be delayed.

You will not achieve healthy grass growth without a good soil base. The pH (acidity) level of the soil must be established in order to choose the most suitable type of fertiliser to use. **The ideal soil pH (acidity) level for grass is pH 6.5**. Analysis of the soil should be carried out every three to four years to ensure the most appropriate fertiliser for your pasture is being used.

FERTILISING

Does your land need fertilising? A low-intensity pasture where the droppings are spread and no hay is taken may need very little fertiliser, and both the horse and sward may well benefit from not applying any. If fertiliser is required, it is advisable to apply a small quantity in the spring, and then again at the start of the 'rest' period, so that it can be absorbed. Allow approximately six weeks before turning the horse onto manure-treated pasture to give time for the excess manure to dry out.

Taking *heavy* agricultural machinery onto the land will damage the soil, and although you can lessen the damage by doing any work when the ground is frozen, the machinery may still cause damage such as soil compaction.

If you are using chemical-based fertilisers, follow the manufacturers' application and resting instructions carefully and seek professional advice if you are unsure.

WHICH FERTILISER TO USE

The vital soil nutrients are lime, potash, phoshate and nitrogen. **Lime** deficiency, indicated by a low soil pH can be adjusted

It also speeds up the decomposition of droppings, minimising rough areas, and will not lower the soil pH, removing the need for an additional dressing of lime. However, because it helps to release nutrients in the same way as lime does, it may have less effect on soil that is already highly alkaline.

Farmyard manure is the most common and economic form of natural, organic fertiliser that provides all the vital nutrients. It must be rotted down for at least six months before spreading.

by applying a treatment of limestone, chalk or calcified seaweed, preferably in autumn or spring. **Potash** is necessary for plant growth. Established levels tend to remain constant on land grazed by horses. **Phosphate** is particularly beneficial on pasture intended for grazing brood mares and youngstock, as is calcium, as both play a part in encouraging healthy bone growth. Many compound fertilisers contain phosphate. Only an occasional application of both phosphate and potash is needed. **Nitrogen** may induce a lush yield of over-rich grass, making it an unsuitable fertiliser for horse pasture.

CLOVER CONTENT

A low clover content suggests low soil phosphate levels. Clover prefers soil with a higher pH.

Calcified Seaweed is completely organic and produces a deliciously sweet crop of grass. It can be applied at any time of year providing it has warmth and moisture for stimulation. It is more useful than farmyard manure because the pasture will not need resting after the application and one application can actually last for many years.

MANURE TIP

Farmyard manure acts more slowly than artificial fertiliser, avoiding flushes of grass commonly associated with chemical fertilisers.

MANURE TIP

Horse manure must not be spread on equine pasture, as it will reintroduce worm larvae to the field.

Poultry manure is less suitable for equine pasture as it is high in nitrogen and will result in flushes of rich grass.

HARROWING

The land may be harrowed once it is dry. **Spiked harrowing** will rejuvenate the pasture by combing, to aerate the soil surface and remove dead grasses. Some pull out pasture-choking weeds such as chickweed, as well as evenly spreading mounds of earth, hillocks and dried manure.

Chain harrowing will aerate the sward, pull out moss, prepare fine seedbeds and level-out surfaces. This is best performed during the summer when the ground is dry and being rested. Chain harrowing while the ground is wet, which is when worm eggs and larvae on the droppings can survive, will risk contaminating the pasture by spreading the moist droppings.

ROLLING

Rolling creates a level surface and can promote early grass growth by raising the soil temperature if done in early spring. Rolling is not recommended on clay or heavy loam soils as it can damage soil structure and create an impervious pan, which will cause problems with drainage and may restrict growth.

A FRESH START

As a sward ages, the original balance of components changes as types of grass are lost due to competition, the environment or management influences. Weeds often spread because they gain control over one or two areas in the field. The spread can be controlled to a point by using an appropriate herbicide to eliminate competition, thereby renovating the sward. Serious consideration

must be given to deciding whether or not to plough and reseed. Good grass is very hard to re-establish, so think carefully about ploughing before you start.

PLOUGHING

If, having assessed the quality of sward and soil, you decide it is necessary to reseed the land, you will first need to plough the land. Remember that ploughing should not be

viewed as a quick and easy alternative to weed control. It is expensive and, if untreated, weeds will be buried to regrow and quickly reinfest the new sward. It is therefore necessary to destroy with an appropriate herbicide, and, if necessary, dig out any existing weeds before ploughing. The field must then be scarified before it can be reseeded.

RESEEDING

The best time to reseed is March or April, when the ground is starting to warm up and dry out. Bringing a tractor onto wet, heavy soil too soon after a wet autumn or winter will cause great damage to the land. Once new grass has grown it is advisable to keep horses off the pasture over the following summer and to graze sheep instead. Sheep will encourage a dense sward. Do not ride on the new grass for at least a year. Horses may be grazed again at the end of the summer but do not allow the ground to become poached. Remove weeds with their roots as soon as they start to grow.

PLANTS

POISONOUS PLANTS

There are many common and widespread plants that, if eaten, will cause poisoning. However, if good grazing is available, they are less likely to be eaten. Please refer to *All About Poisonous Plants* by Sonia Davidson (J. A. Allen) for a more detailed guide. For the purposes of general field management, I have selected the most common or dangerous plants that must be eradicated and removed from horse pasture.

Ragwort is highly poisonous and resistant to treatment. The most widespread species is common ragwort (*Senecio jacobea*). Young plants at the early rosette stage (*right*) may only be

10–15 cm (4–6 in) so a careful examination of the field must be made daily, as new growth is remarkably rapid.

Mature plants grow to a height of 90–120 cm (3–4 ft) and have bright yellow flowers (*see lower photo*).

An eradication programme may take several years, as each plant is capable of producing up to 100 new ones, and seeds can lie dormant in the soil for 20 years. The most effective method is to spray young rosettes with a recommended herbicide in April to early June. *Do not* graze the pasture again until the treated plants have died, disintegrated, been dug out and cleared from the field. Avoid dumping the treated plants near the field, particularly in accessible areas. Cutting should only be used as an emergency measure to prevent flowering and seeding.

Yew (*Taxus baccata*) poisoning may result in death a few hours after any part of the yew is eaten. (*See below.*)

BEWARE

Remember that ragwort is poisonous to sheep and cattle, as well as horses.

Oak (*Querus spp*) poisoning is most likely during the spring, when buds and young leaves may be eaten, and in the autumn, when acorns drop to the ground and will be dangerous if eaten in large quantities. (*See right.*)

Bracken (*Pteridium aquilinum*) poisoning will occur if any part of the plant is eaten, even after cutting and drying. The roots are thought to be more poisonous than the fronds, so take care when ploughing land upon which bracken is growing, especially between August and October when the fronds are turning brown (*see right*).

Privet, box, laburnum and **laurel** are poisonous but are not normally eaten. They are often used to make complete domestic hedges and are also found in field hedges. They become more appetising to the horse when they are dead.

OTHER PLANTS

There are a number of weeds, which although not poisonous, have no nutritional value, and will rapidly take over the pasture if allowed to seed or spread.

The most common of these are daisies, docks, chickweed and broad-leaved plantain. These can be easily pulled up but docks may require treating in the same way as ragwort to minimise regrowth.

Some plants, such as nettles, thistles and dandelions, will be enjoyed by the horse when cut, and have many herbal benefits but, again, they will spread quickly and should not be encouraged in equine pasture.

USEFUL HERBS

A herb-rich pasture may provide a combination of nutrients and will be more beneficial to the horse than a monoculture pasture. However, little is actually known about this at present. Palatable herbs often found in pastures include: yarrow, dandelion and ribwort.

BUTTERCUPS

There are many species of buttercup, some of which are poisonous to horses and all spread rapidly (*see below*). The poisonous species contain a substance that causes blistering when chewed and may lead to excessive salivating, colic and diarrhoea, depending on how much the horse has eaten. It is advisable to treat buttercups as you would any other poisonous plant.

FIELD SECURITY

FENCING AND BOUNDARIES

Hedges at a height of about 1.2–1.5 m (4–5 ft) provide suitable boundaries if kept tidy and dense. Ask a farmer to cut the hedge back each year to prevent its outward spread. This will also maximise the grazing area by making more of the field accessible to the horse. If the hedge is thin in parts, use an additional type of fencing such as post and rail. Ensure the hedge is tidy and free from poisonous evergreens.

Post and rail is the most traditional form of fencing and is easy to maintain. Wood should be treated regularly with preservative or paint. Make daily checks for broken rails and perform repairs immediately. Posts should preferably be 1.5 m (5 ft) (or at least 1.4 m [4 ft 6 in]) and erected ideally 1.2 m (4 ft) above and 30 cm (1 ft) below the ground.

Plastic fencing is strong and safe and is made from plastic or PVC-u strips which are erected either on wooden or plastic posts. It is strong and durable, so

will not rot, split or suffer chewing damage like a wooden fence, and requires little or no maintenance. Installation instructions depend on the manufacturer.

Electric fencing, whether temporary or permanent, is economical, secure, effective and incredibly quick and easy to install and move around. It can be used for many purposes such as dividing the pasture for rotation, to separate or isolate certain horses, to reinforce existing fencing or to restrict access to certain areas. There are many different types of electric fencing available so choose the one that suits your needs. Follow the individual manufacturer's instructions for installation.

Plain wire is a very economical type of fencing providing it is firmly erected and pulled tight. It can be made more solid and visible by erecting a rail at the top. Use a line of electric fence in between the rows of plain wire to prevent horses stretching the wire as they lean through the fence.

High-tensile steel wire is extremely robust but can be dangerous if the horse injures himself on the wire.

Walls and banks are used as field boundaries in certain parts of the country. Additional fencing may be required to keep stock secure. As with any fencing, walls must be of an adequate height and be regularly checked for signs of damage. (*See below and opposite above.*)

UNSUITABLE FENCING

Barbed wire may be cheap and secure but it is not recommended owing to the risk of injury and the possibility of a horse's head-collar getting caught on the barbs. Rugs are also likely to be damaged if snagged on the wire. The photo below shows an extremely dangerous fence. The barbed wire is rusty which could cause a nasty injury. There is only one strand of wire and this is far too low which could encourage the horse to step over it thus increasing the chance of injury.

Wire mesh or **stock netting** is durable, secure, and useful for grazing horses with sheep or cattle, but be aware that a horse may put his feet through the fence and become caught in the wire, particularly if it is not kept taut or if the mesh contains holes or tears.

RAIL INJURIES

Iron rails are likely to inflict nasty injuries.

Chestnut fencing (*above*) is made from cleft chestnut pales that are unsuitable for equine use.

GATES

Wooden gates should ideally be made from oak as it is long lasting and does not warp. Cheaper softwood may warp and will break more easily. All timber will last

longer if treated with preservative. Gate-posts should be made from oak, set 90 cm (3 ft) in the ground and hard-rammed with stone or set in concrete.

Metal gates (*see below*) must be heavy duty to avoid hazardous fractures or breaks and regularly treated with rust-resistant paint. Posts can be metal or timber and should, again, be set in concrete.

Fastenings should be secure and with no dangerous edges. Hinges should be strong and made from galvanised steel. Gates should be hung so that they open easily and clear the ground when opened.

Padlocks are advisable to prevent horses being stolen or learning to open the gate fastenings. The gate can be made more secure by putting an extra chain and padlock around the hinge end to prevent it from being opened by being lifted off the hinges.

A DANGEROUS GATEWAY

This gate is rusty and not hung properly which makes it difficult and potentially dangerous to open. In addition, the surrounding fence is made up of makeshift bits of fencing.

FIELD AMENITIES

WATER AND WATER TROUGHS

A constant supply of fresh, clean water should be readily available. A horse's health may deteriorate rapidly if he is deprived of fresh water. Troughs should be sited in a well-drained area of the field, away from trees which will dirty the water, and positioned so that it projects as little as possible. It should be set on solid brick or concrete supports and surrounded by hardcore to prevent the ground around it becoming poached.

If a bucket is used, a large, heavy-duty water bucket should be sufficient for one horse. Look for designs (*see below*) featuring two layers to prevent freezing during icy weather. For more than one horse, a livestock water trough will be needed. These vary in size and are usually made from galvanised steel or high-density polythene.

WATER TRANSPORT

If there is no water supply to the field, transport water easily and without spills using a water carrier.

WATER FEATURE

Concrete troughs are permanent and more expensive.

Galvanised steel troughs are ideal. These should be approximately 1–2 m (3–6 ft) long, about 38 cm (15 ins) deep and set so that the top is about 60 cm (2 ft) from the ground. This should be checked twice daily and kept clear of debris, ice and leaves.

A covered ballcock will detect when the water supply is decreasing and will drop to allow more water to flow. Daily inspection of the ballcock system and trough is advisable.

Some people use old household baths as inexpensive water troughs. Make sure there are no sharp projecting edges or cracks before use. Taps should be out of the horse's reach. All troughs must be regularly scrubbed clean and the water changed.

In freezing weather, all exposed piping should be lagged and boarded and the cavity filled with fibreglass. Ice should be broken when necessary to allow the horse to drink. Putting a football in the trough in freezing weather will ensure that there is always an unfrozen patch in the frozen water.

NATURAL LAGGING

Cover any exposed piping with hot horse manure. Then, cover this with well-secured plastic sheeting. The manure can be replaced with fresh manure as necessary.

SHELTER

Shelter is vital to enable the horse to shelter from harsh winter weather or hot sun and flies. Dense overhanging trees or hedges will provide adequate natural shelter. If natural shelter is not available, a strongly constructed field shelter with a well-drained floor and thick bed should be provided. Site the shelter against or away from the fence, with the rear side facing the prevailing wind.

DAILY AND LONG-TERM MANAGEMENT

DAILY CHECKS

Check for:
- droppings (check the field shelter if applicable);
- poisonous plants;
- litter;
- rabbit holes;
- rough, uneven ground;
- fencing;
- clean water supply;
- availability of shelter.

This photo illustrates poor field management.

LONG-TERM MANAGEMENT OBJECTIVES

Now that a healthy sward suitable for equine grazing has been established, you must work constantly to maintain it. Your main aims should include:

- maintaining a healthy dense sward;
- keeping the land free from droppings;
- keeping the land free from dangerous or rapidly spreading problem plants (the Weeds Act 1959 makes it an offence for an occupier of any land not to remove or prevent the spread of 'injurious weeds' [thistle, docks and ragwort] from that land);
- keeping the land free from litter or other dangerous objects, and maintaining all fencing and gates.

ACKNOWLEDGEMENTS

Thanks to my father for pursuing me around the countryside, camera at the ready, in search of a multitude of weeds and poisonous plants. Thank you to the many people who allowed me to photograph their horses, livestock and property, and to the following companies for assisting with the photography:

Drivall Ltd.	(electric fencing)	Tel: 0121 423 1122
Duralock (UK) Ltd.	(PVC-u fencing)	Tel: 01752 484085
Logic Manufacturing Ltd.	(atv equipment)	Tel: 01434 606661
Monsanto Plc	(Roundup Biactive weedkiller)	Tel: 01494 613123
Withington Hill Stables	(field shelter)	Tel: 0161 427 1209

(Telephone numbers correct at time of going to print)

British Library Cataloguing-in-Publication Data.
A catalogue record for this book is available from the British Library

ISBN 0.85131.818.5

© Sian Evans 2001

Published in Great Britain in 2001 by
J. A. Allen an imprint of Robert Hale Ltd.,
Clerkenwell House, 45–47 Clerkenwell Green,
London EC1R 0HT

Reprinted 2003

Design and Typesetting by Paul Saunders
Series editor Jane Lake
Colour processing by Tenon & Polert Colour Processing Ltd., Hong Kong
Printed in Malta by Gutenberg Press Ltd.